SCIENCE
in Action

THE HUMAN BODY

YOUR
HEART AND
LUNGS

Sally Hewitt

Quarto Library

Publisher: Maxime Boucknooghe
Editorial Director: Victoria Garrard
Art Director: Miranda Snow
Series Editor: Claudia Martin
Series Designer: Bruce Marshall
Photographer: Michael Wicks
Illustrator: Chris Davidson
Consultant: Kristina Routh

This library edition published in 2016 by Quarto Library., an imprint of QEB Publishing, Inc.

6 Orchard, Lake Forest, CA 92630

© 2016 QEB Publishing,
Published by Quarto Library., an imprint of Quarto Publishing Group USA Inc.

Distributed in the United States and Canada by
Lerner Publisher Services
241 First Avenue North
Minneapolis, MN 55401 U.S.A.
www.lernerbooks.com

A CIP record for the book is available from the Library of Congress.

ISBN 978 1 60992 879 7

Printed in China

Words in **bold** can be found in the glossary on page 22.

Contents

Your amazing heart

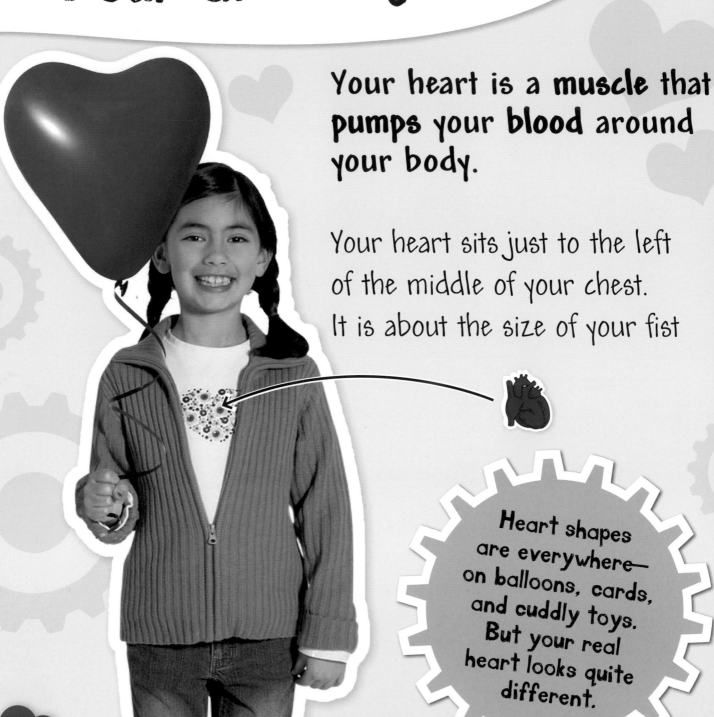

Your heart is a **muscle** that **pumps** your **blood** around your body.

Your heart sits just to the left of the middle of your chest. It is about the size of your fist

Heart shapes are everywhere—on balloons, cards, and cuddly toys. But your real heart looks quite different.

A doctor listens to your heart pumping in your chest using a stethoscope.

Your heart is always working. It pumps blood all day and night to all the different parts of your body. Every part of your body—your brain, **lungs**, skin, etc— needs blood to keep it working properly.

Your heart doesn't need to work as hard when you are asleep. It has to beat faster when you wake up and start moving.

Heartbeat

Your heart muscle squeezes over and over again giving a heart "beat".

When your heart fills up with blood, the heart muscle squeezes to push this blood out into your **blood vessels**. Your heart then fills up with more blood.

Activity

When you're next in the bath, try filling a rubber duck, squeezy bath toy or even a plastic bottle with water, then squeezing it out. Do it again... and again! This is like your heart muscles squeezing as it pumps blood.

Be careful where you squirt the water!

6

Each side of your heart has two rooms or "chambers".
The right side of your heart pumps blood into your lungs
to collect **oxygen**. The left side pumps this blood back into
your body.

To body

To lungs

Two left
chambers

Two right
chambers

Veins and arteries

Your heart pumps your blood into tubes called blood vessels.

Blood vessels called arteries carry blood away from your heart to every part of your body. Blood vessels called veins bring blood back to your heart.

Arteries (red)

Veins (blue)

When you get hot, your skin may turn red. This is because blood rushes to the blood vessels in your skin to keep you cool.

8

Blood is constantly moving around your body. This movement is called circulation. It takes less than a minute for your heart to pump blood to every part of your body!

Activity

Hold your left hand in the air for a few moments. Hang your right hand down by your side. Now look at the color of each hand.

It is harder for your heart to pump blood upward, so your left hand looks pale because there is less blood in it. It is easy for blood to flow downward, so your right hand is more red.

Blood

Your blood carries oxygen from your lungs, and goodness from your food, all around your body.

Your blood is full of tiny cells that carry oxygen. These cells give your blood its red color.

If you cut yourself, your blood dries into a hard scab. Your skin then heals underneath the scab.

When your body is working hard, if you are running for example, it needs more oxygen from your blood. This means your heart beats faster.

You can feel your heartbeat by placing your fingers on the blood vessels on your wrists. This is called your pulse.

Activity

Feel your pulse. Now run in place for a few moments. Feel your pulse again.

Your heart usually beats about 90 times a minute.

Your pulse gets faster when you work hard.

Lungs

You use your lungs to **breathe** in air.
They are like two big balloons.

Nose

Mouth

Windpipe

Ribs

Lungs

To leave enough room for your heart, your left lung is a bit smaller than your right lung. Your lungs are protected by your ribs.

Your lungs are like sponges. They have lots of tiny bubbles which fill with air.

Oxygen is a gas in the air. Your body needs oxygen to stay alive, so you need to breathe air in and out of your lungs all the time.

▲ Humans can't breathe underwater, unless they use a tube called a snorkel!

Breathe in...

You use your mouth and nose to breathe in air. Air goes down your **windpipe** into your lungs and they get bigger as they fill up.

Tiny hairs in your nose and windpipe catch bits of dirt to make the air going into your lungs as clean as possible.

Oxygen from the air goes into tiny blood vessels in your lungs. Blood full of oxygen flows to your heart and your heart pumps it around your body.

Every day, the average person breathes in around 2,900 gallons (11,000 liters) of air. That's enough to fill a small swimming pool!

Breathe out...

After your lungs have taken oxygen from the air, you breathe out.

The stale air goes up your windpipe and out through your mouth and nose.

Activity

Put your hand near your mouth and breathe on it. Your breath feels warm.

The air you breathe out gets warm as it goes through your body.

When you breathe out on a cold day, you see the tiny drops of water in your breath like a cloud.

The air you breathe in is full of oxygen. The air you breathe out is full of a gas called carbon dioxide. Your body does not need carbon dioxide, so you get rid of it. Your breath also has tiny drops of water in it.

Sneezing gets rid of things your body doesn't want to breathe in. Fast!

17

Talking

You need your lungs to talk as well as to breathe. You speak and sing with a part of your windpipe called your voice box.

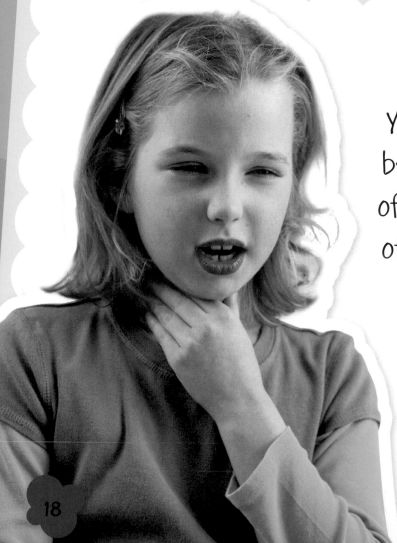

Activity

You can feel your voice box by gently touching the front of your neck. Make all kinds of different sounds—shout, screech, and whisper. Does your voice box move when you make a sound?

You make sounds when air flows over folds of muscle called "vocal cords" in your voice box. The more air that goes over the folds, the louder the sounds!

▶ Shouting uses lots of air. When you shout, you soon get out of breath.

Hiccupping is when air rushes in and hits your voice box.

Healthy heart and lungs

You need to look after your heart and lungs. Keeping active makes your heart and lungs work harder and this helps to keep your whole body strong and healthy.

Healthy eating

You can protect your heart and lungs by eating fresh food, lots of fruit and vegetables, and not too much fat, salt, or sugar.

Healthy food is good for you and delicious too!

Fresh air

Fresh air is good for your lungs. Sometimes the air in big cities is polluted by fumes from cars. Polluted air contains tiny bits of smoke and dust that enter your lungs and make you cough.

▲ Air is cleaner in the countryside and at the seaside.

Sleep

When you sleep, your brain keeps you breathing without you having to think about it.

When you wake up after a good night's sleep, you are rested and ready to start the day.

GLOSSARY

Blood

Blood is red liquid that runs through your blood vessels to every part of your body. It carries goodness from your food and oxygen from your lungs.

Blood vessels

Blood vessels are tubes that carry your blood. Arteries are blood vessels that carry blood away from your heart. Veins are blood vessels that carry blood back to your heart.

Breathe

You breathe air in and out of your lungs all the time. You breathe through your nose and mouth.

Muscle

Your muscles pull your bones so you can move. Muscles keep your heart beating and your lungs breathing.

Lungs

Lungs are the part of your body you breathe with. They take oxygen from the air and pass it to your blood.

Oxygen

Oxygen is a gas in the air. Your lungs take oxygen from the air when you breathe in. Your blood carries oxygen from your lungs all around your body. Every part of your body needs oxygen to stay alive.

Pump

A pump pushes liquid along. Your heart is a pump that pushes blood through your blood vessels.

Windpipe

Your windpipe is the tube that carries air into your lungs when you breathe in, and carries it out again when you breathe out.

INDEX

NEXT STEPS

* Show the children the position of your heart, just to the left and middle of your chest. Make a fist to show the size of your heart. An adult's fist is bigger than a child's fist. Talk about the comparative size of a child's heart and an adult's heart.

* Feel your ribs and breastbone. Discuss how your ribs protect your heart. Explain that your heart needs to be protected because it is soft. Use the word "muscle" and ask the children to point out other muscles that let them move. Use the word "pump" and talk about how a pump pushes liquid.

* Talk about how blood travels through blood vessels in the same way that water travels through pipes. Ask the children to find pipes around the home.

* Feel each other's pulse and explain that each beat is your heart pumping blood all around your body.

* Breathe in and out through your nose and mouth. Try putting your hand in front of your face. Feel air coming out of your nose. Now feel it coming out of your mouth. Ask the children if they think air comes out of both their nose and their mouth at the same time.

* Run together on the spot and feel how your heart beats faster and you breathe more quickly after exercise. Explain that this is because your body needs more oxygen when you work hard. Feel your heart beat and ask the children what they notice about their breathing when they rest.